WHO ARE THE COVID-19 HELPERS?

By Sara Latta

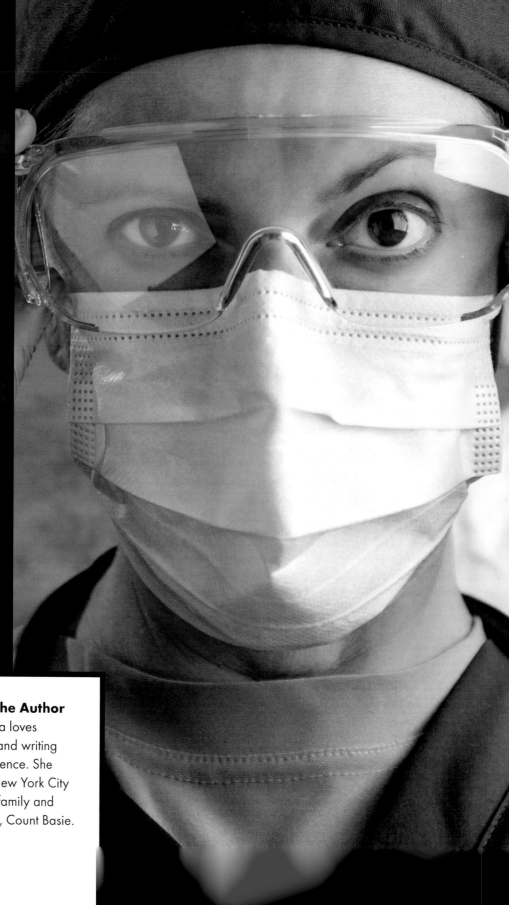

The Child's World®
childsworld.com

Published by The Child's World®
1980 Lookout Drive
Mankato, MN 56003-1705
800-599-READ
www.childsworld.com

Photos ©: Alexandros Michailidis/
Shutterstock.com: 19; Andy
Dean Photography/Shutterstock.
com: cover, 2; eldar nurkovic/
Shutterstock.com: 9; faboi/
Shutterstock.com: 15; Jes Farnum/
Shutterstock.com: 6; Maridav/
Shutterstock.com: 13; Mongkolchon
Akesin/Shutterstock.com: 5;
peenat/Shutterstock.com: 20;
pixfly/Shutterstock.com: 10;
theskaman306/Shutterstock.com:
16; Veja/Shutterstock.com: 22

ISBN 9781503853157
(Reinforced Library Binding)

ISBN 9781503853249
(Portable Document Format)

ISBN 9781503853300
(Online Multi-user eBook)

LCCN: 2020939106

Printed in the United
States of America

About the Author

Sara Latta loves reading and writing about science. She lives in New York City with her family and their dog, Count Basie.

CONTENTS

CHAPTER ONE

Look for the Helpers

There is a new disease called COVID-19. The name stands for "**CO**rona **VI**rus **D**isease 20**19**." It started in the year 2019. It has caused lots of sickness and even death. That might make you feel scared. That's okay. A man named Fred Rogers taught us that when things feel scary, we should "look for the helpers."

There are many helpers who are working to keep people safe and healthy. Let's get to know some of them.

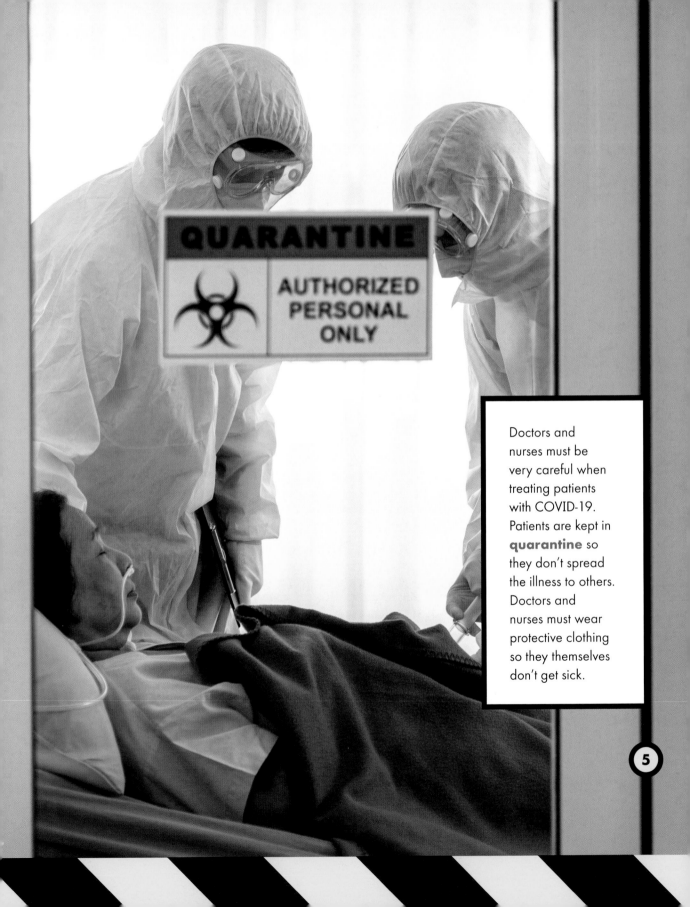

Doctors and nurses must be very careful when treating patients with COVID-19. Patients are kept in **quarantine** so they don't spread the illness to others. Doctors and nurses must wear protective clothing so they themselves don't get sick.

Bus drivers help other workers get from place to place during COVID-19.

We are all doing our best to make sure the **virus** does not spread. Everyone is staying close to home if they can. Some grownups can work from home. You may be going to school at home.

Not everyone can stay at home. Bus drivers take workers to their jobs across towns and cities. Train conductors guide subway riders from station to station. Taxi drivers take people to see the doctor. They are all **essential** workers. They wear masks and gloves to keep themselves and others safe. You can help the helpers by wearing a mask if you ride with them.

COVID-19 FACT

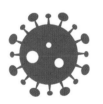

COVID-19 is caused by a type of virus called a coronavirus. Viruses are tiny germs that can make us sick. They are too small to see without a powerful microscope.

The garbage truck rumbles by. Workers jump out and haul bags of trash into the back of the truck. Street cleaning trucks whir by, sucking up small bits of trash. Janitors keep the insides of buildings nice and clean. Think of how dirty our streets and buildings would be without these important helpers.

Hear the firetruck? Firefighters rush to put out fires. They rescue people from burning buildings. Police officers are out on the street too. They look out for people in trouble. They help keep us safe. They are all helpers.

COVID-19 FACT

In some parts of the country, school bus drivers have a new job. Instead of driving kids to school, they are delivering meals to the families of children on their routes.

Some essential workers must wear protective masks very tightly and for long periods of time. This often marks their faces for a while.

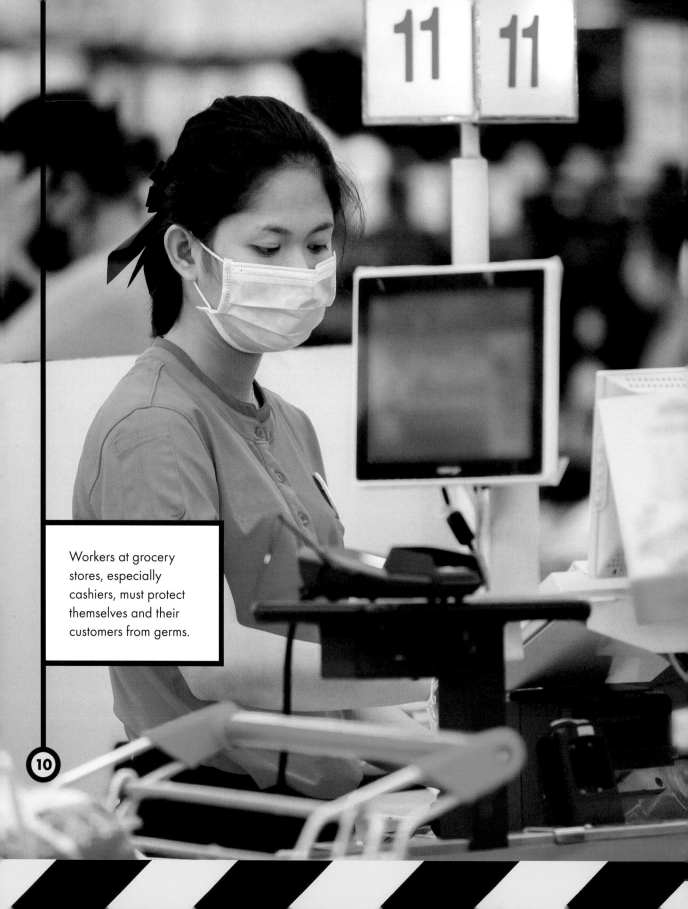

Workers at grocery stores, especially cashiers, must protect themselves and their customers from germs.

CHAPTER TWO

Who Helps Put Food On Our Tables?

Farmers and farm workers go to work every day to grow and harvest our fruits and vegetables. They milk the cows. They feed the chickens and gather the eggs. The good food we eat begins with the farm helpers!

Workers at factories prepare the farmers' food so it can be sent to grocery stores. They often have to work close together. These helpers wear masks and gloves to protect themselves and the other workers.

At the grocery stores, workers stock the shelves with cereal, juice, and all kinds of good food. Clerks bag the groceries. Grocery store helpers are around a lot of people, all day long. They, too, wear masks and gloves to protect themselves from infection.

Some helpers work in food pantries or meal programs. They give food to people for free. No one should ever have to go hungry, even when people are afraid of getting sick.

COVID-19 FACT

When lots of people were getting sick from COVID-19, some restaurants started sending free food to health care helpers in the hospitals.

People delivering everything from groceries to packages are important during COVID-19. They help keep the disease from spreading by letting more people stay at home.

Restaurant cooks make pizza, sandwiches, and other yummy food. Even though you may not be able to sit down and eat inside, you can pick up the food and eat it at home. Many restaurants also deliver their food.

The delivery workers are helpers too! Some delivery helpers bring us food from restaurants and grocery stores. Postal carriers bring us mail and packages.

CHAPTER THREE

Who Keeps Us Healthy?

If someone needs to get to the hospital quickly, there is a phone number to call: 9-1-1. The helper who answers the phone can call an **ambulance**. An ambulance is a van used to carry people who are sick or injured. They can take people to hospitals.

Specially trained helpers called **paramedics** respond to the calls. They give sick or injured people the care they need until they can get to the hospital.

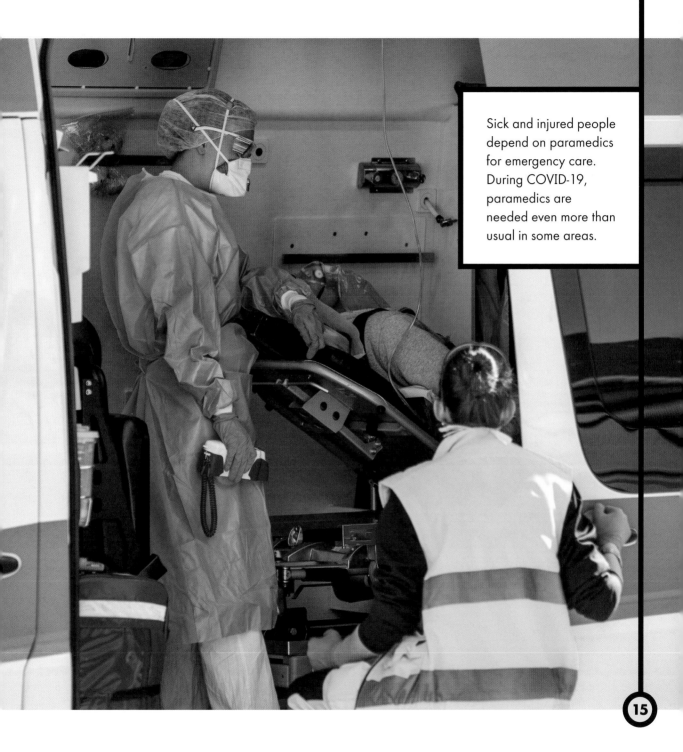

Sick and injured people depend on paramedics for emergency care. During COVID-19, paramedics are needed even more than usual in some areas.

Doctors and nurses must protect themselves from germs. They must also protect their patients from additional germs which could make them even more sick.

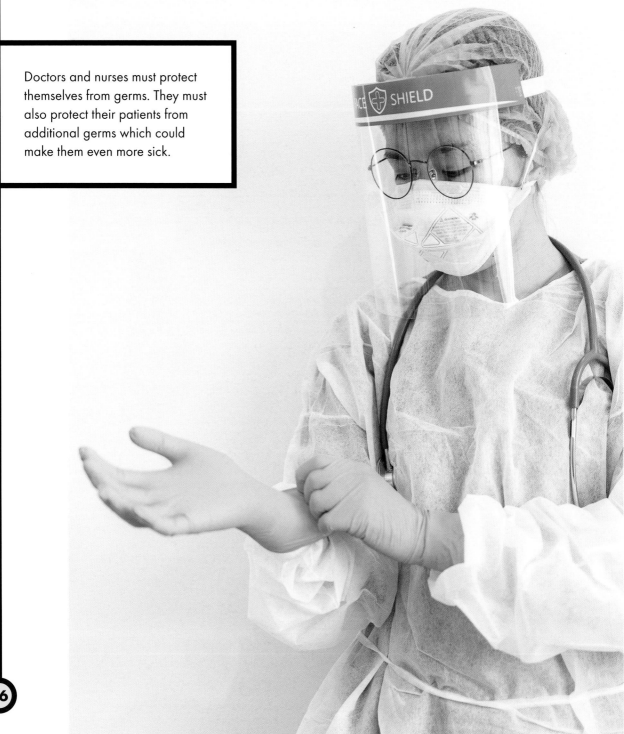

At the hospital or clinic, nurses and other helpers care for people who are so sick with COVID-19 that it is no longer safe for them to stay at home. They care for others who are sick or injured too. They work hard to prevent the spread of the virus. They may wear masks, shields that cover their faces, booties, and paper gowns to keep themselves safe.

Some nurses and helpers work in nursing homes. These are places where people who are elderly or unable to take care of themselves can live. The virus can make older people or people who have other illnesses sicker than others. This may mean their families can't come to visit. Nursing home helpers can work to bring families together by telephone or video.

Doctors work closely with nurses to treat patients sick with COVID-19. They ask their patients questions about how they feel. They decide what medicines are best. Sometimes they give patients more oxygen through a tube in their nose to help them breathe better.

Disease detectives study how people get sick with COVID-19 and how to stop the spread of the virus. They discover how far the virus can travel when you cough, sneeze, or even sing. These helpers tell us when we need to stay at home. They can also tell us when it is safe to go back to school or the playground.

COVID-19 FACT

The virus that causes COVID-19 is highly **contagious**. Keeping at least six feet (2 meters) from other people helps stop the virus's spread.

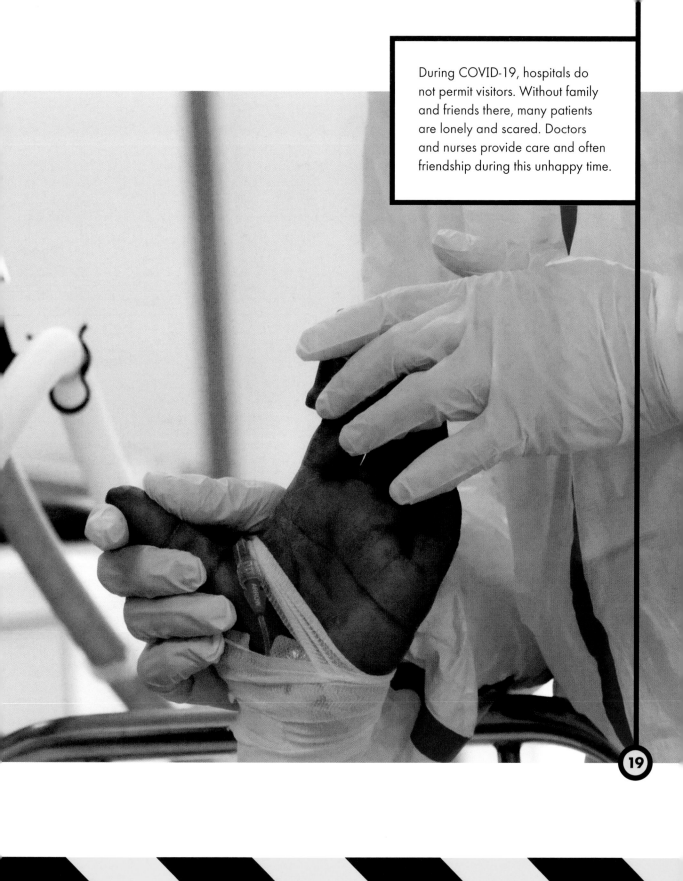

During COVID-19, hospitals do not permit visitors. Without family and friends there, many patients are lonely and scared. Doctors and nurses provide care and often friendship during this unhappy time.

19

Scientists are testing new medicines that will help people sick with COVID-19. They are working hard to find a coronavirus **vaccine** that will prevent you from getting sick, like the shots you get for other diseases.

THINK ABOUT IT

You can be a helper too! Here are some tips on how you can help keep yourself and others safe.

1. Wear a cloth or paper mask when you go out.

2. Cover your cough or sneeze into a tissue.

3. Wash your hands often with soapy water for 20 seconds. That's about as long as it takes to sing the ABC song—not too fast!

GOOD NEWS!

In many cities across the United States, people are celebrating the helpers at 7 p.m. That is the time when many medical workers end their workday. People open their windows or step out onto their doorsteps to clap and cheer. Some ring bells or sing. It makes everyone feel a little bit happier—especially the helpers.

GLOSSARY

ambulance (AM-byoo-lenss) An ambulance is a specialized vehicle that is used to carry sick or very injured people to the hospital.

contagious (kun-TAY-juss) When something is contagious, it spreads easily from person to person.

essential (ih-SEN-chull) Something that is essential is very important. Some types of workers are essential.

paramedic (payr-uh-MED-ik) A paramedic is a specially trained person who helps sick or injured people before and while they are being taken to the hospital.

quarantine (KWOR-un-teen) To be in quarantine is to stay away from others to avoid spreading illness.

vaccine (vak-SEEN) A vaccine is a weakened or dead form of a disease that is swallowed or injected into a person. This causes their body to fight the germs, and gives them the ability to fight that disease's germs if the body comes in contact with them again.

virus (VY-russ) A virus is a very tiny organism that causes diseases. A virus can only be seen with a special kind of microscope.

TO LEARN MORE

IN THE LIBRARY

Hegarty, Patricia. *Thank You, Helpers: Doctors, Nurses, Teachers, Grocery Workers, and More Who Care for Us*. New York, NY: Random House, 2020.

Latta, Sara. *What Is COVID-19?* Mankato, MN: The Child's World, 2021.

Wallace, Adam M. *The Day My Kids Stayed Home: Explaining COVID-19 and the Corona Virus to Your Kids*. Adam M. Wallace, 2020.

ON THE WEB

Visit our website for links about COVID-19:

childsworld.com/links

Note to Parents, Teachers, and Librarians: We routinely verify our Web links to make sure they are safe and active sites. So encourage your readers to check them out!

INDEX